GEMOLOG

T0158231

Street Jewellery Styles & Styling Tips

Liza Urla

Photographed by
Julia Flit & Liza Urla

GEMOLOGUE

Street Jewellery Styles & Styling Tips

Liza Urla

Photographed by
Julia Flit & Liza Urla

ACC Art Books

BIO

Liza Urla is a jewellery curator, writer, stylist and creative muse, devoting her time to the things that inspire her, living and travelling all over the world. Her jewellery influence has been acknowledged by the *Financial Times, Vogue* and *Harper's Bazaar.*

Initially, to satisfy her passion for jewellery, Liza Urla just wanted to take photographs of jewellery on people she came across in different cities. She founded GEMOLOGUE in 2009 to celebrate jewellery and to showcase her precious discoveries from all over the world. Since then, it has become a leading and much-loved jewellery destination and blog.

Julia Flit is a London-based jewellery and fashion photographer. She has travelled the world, capturing with her camera some of the best international jewellery designers. She has been working with GEMOLOGUE for several years, and this book would not have happened without her.

I never look at the eyes first, instead I look at the jewellery. I notice jewellery from the corner of my eye as people are passing by. I have always been absolutely fascinated by jewellery, how people wear it and why. Jewellery is the ultimate means of self-expression.

In human history, jewellery came before clothes. It was the first type of adornment. The oldest known pieces are 100,000-year-old beads made from *Nassarius* shells. Jewellery is essential to our identity as humans.

Through GEMOLOGUE, I have been sharing my jewellery journey across many cultures with my audience over the last seven years. I carefully pick pieces that catch my eye and capture my heart. Throughout my jewellery career I have looked at thousands and thousands of jewellery pieces, and this book contains the crème de la crème of what I have seen and experienced.

GEMOLOGUE started as a beautiful anthology of jewellery street style images, as I could not photograph jewellery directly. At the time, jewellery designers were afraid that by posting their images online, their work would be copied. I have been lucky enough to have unique and privileged access to people's jewellery boxes: the best pieces are always in private collections.

Every jewel has a sentimental story attached to it. Every jewel worn has a meaning. In that sense, jewellery is superior to clothes.

This book brings together my favourite images. It includes photographs of people whose jewellery demanded a closer look, juxtaposed against my jewellery styling in collaboration with various designers in the jungle of Brazil, on the beaches of Mexico, or on the streets of London, NYC, Paris or Moscow.

My taste in jewellery is eclectic and I am in love with all types of jewellery, be it fashion, vintage or fine. Jewellery is our armour, and precious stones our amulets. I am a curator of jewellery, and I would always try pieces on before recommending them to my friends and readers.

The purpose of this book is to inspire your jewellery style and to expand your horizons of what jewellery is. I hope that by looking at the images in this book, you will see jewellery in a different light and understand that it has a much wider definition than gold and diamonds.

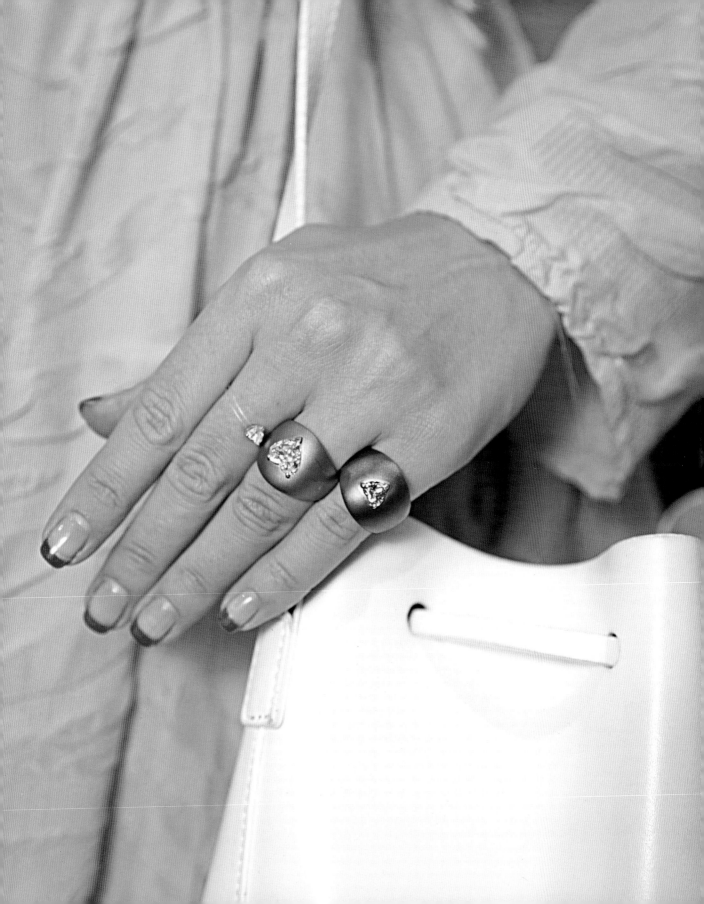

Brooch it up! The most overlooked piece of jewellery. A brooch can add an instant touch of chic to your outfit. Pin a brooch to your favourite masculine blazer to add some feminine flair. Do not be afraid to attach it to a more unusual place... perhaps in place of the top button of your shirt, your hat, or your skirt. Combine a few small brooches for a unique and whimsical look – but keep to the same style, for example, art deco or pop art.

Don't forget to put your jewellery on! Jewellery never fails to lift the spirits. Keep it close at hand, in a visible place. Put necklaces on the same hangers as matching dresses, keep it next to your make-up and perfumes. Jewellery is essential to finishing off your look – DO NOT LEAVE THE HOUSE WITHOUT IT. Put a daily reminder on your phone. Pick out your everyday jewels that you can wear while sleeping or taking a bath.

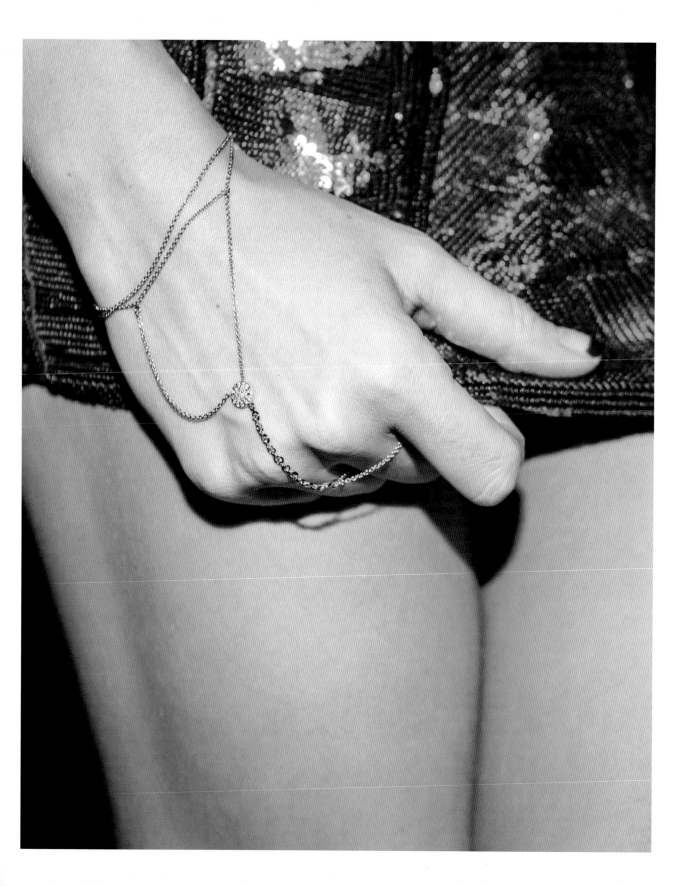

Collect jewellery on your travels. Jewels obviously make the best souvenirs, as well as supporting local craftsmen. Learn the story and traditions behind each piece. Jewellery from foreign lands will always be unique and full of wonderful memories.

Be comfortable in your jewellery. Try to
define your jewellery style: is it classic,
edgy, contemporary, minimal? The jewellery
world is vibrant and never fails to surprise.
Be experimental, but don't go outside your
comfort zone with your purchases.

Celebrate your achievements with a beautiful jewel. Reward yourself. Sophia Loren says in her autobiography *Yesterday, Today, Tomorrow*: 'Each piece had reminded me not only of the movies I'd worked on, but of all the emotions at the time. I could relive everything by wearing a necklace around my neck or a ring on my finger.'

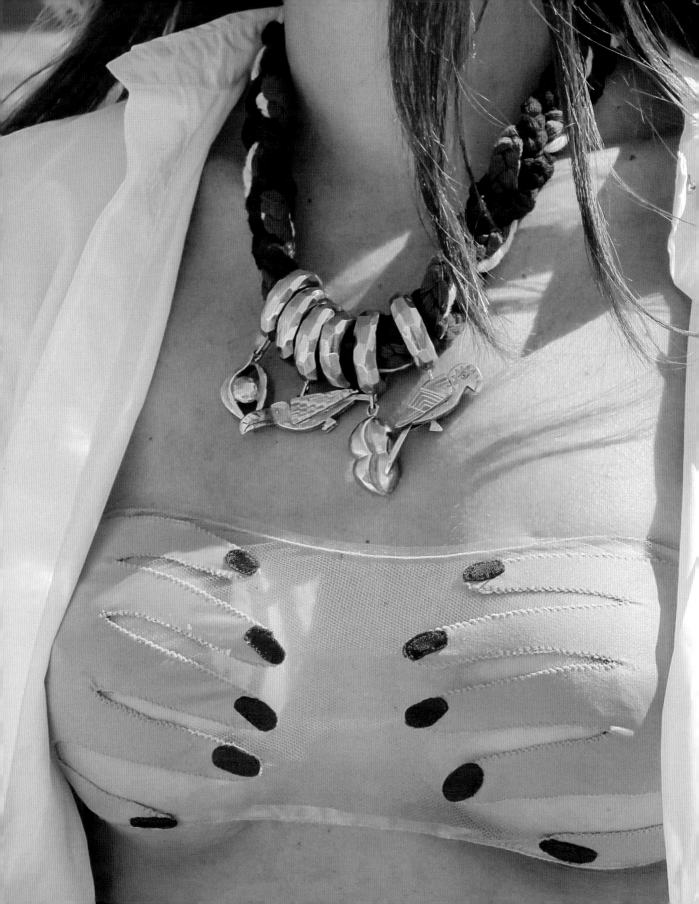

Put together your own one-of-a-kind pendant necklace: an easy way to update your current look. Search for key personal ingredients around your abode - small rings, pearls, charms, gifts from your loved one, family heirlooms, purchases to mark milestones, which you have accumulated over the years - and assemble them onto a long chain. This will be your most personal piece of jewellery.

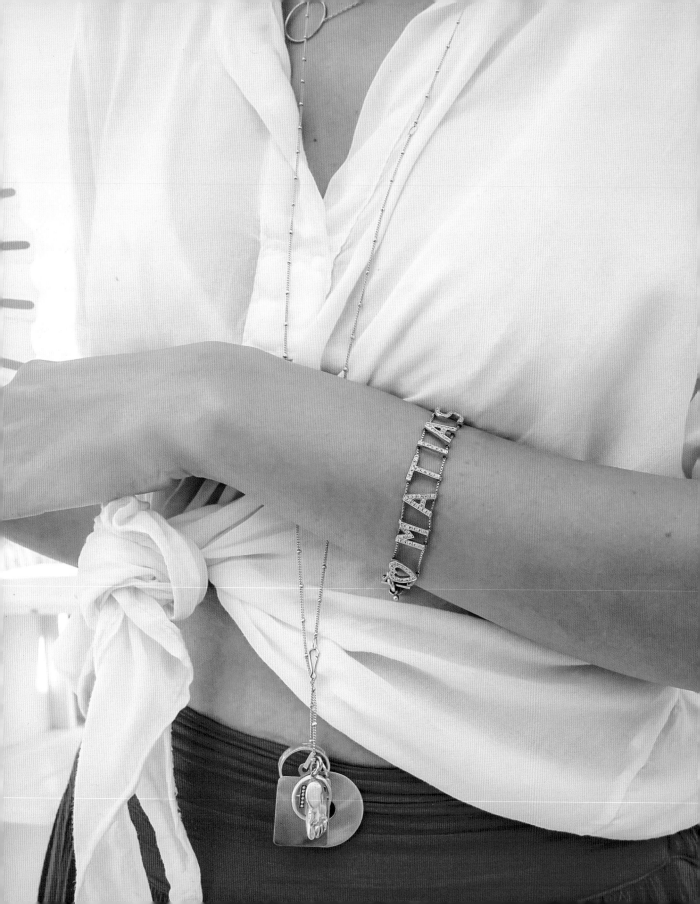

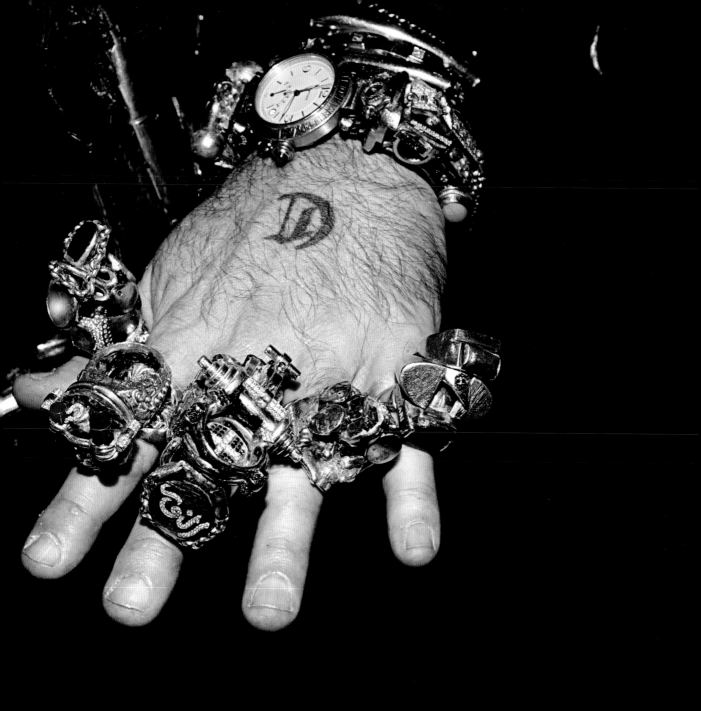

Add some kitsch to your look with striking, whimsical pieces of jewellery. Sometimes jewellery should simply be fun and allow you to express the playful aspect of your personality. A kitsch piece will certainly be a great conversation starter!

Pearls are often considered old-fashioned, but I love them for their pure beauty, symmetry, shape, and a touch of nostalgia. Layer several pearl necklaces as a tribute to the one-and-only Coco Chanel, who is famous for her look incorporating several strands of splendid white pearls.

Jewellery has a rich social and cultural history. It has been around for thousands of years, and worn by humans even before clothes. Draw inspiration from museums and their spectacular collections of jewellery: ancient, medieval, Renaissance or perhaps something a little more contemporary.

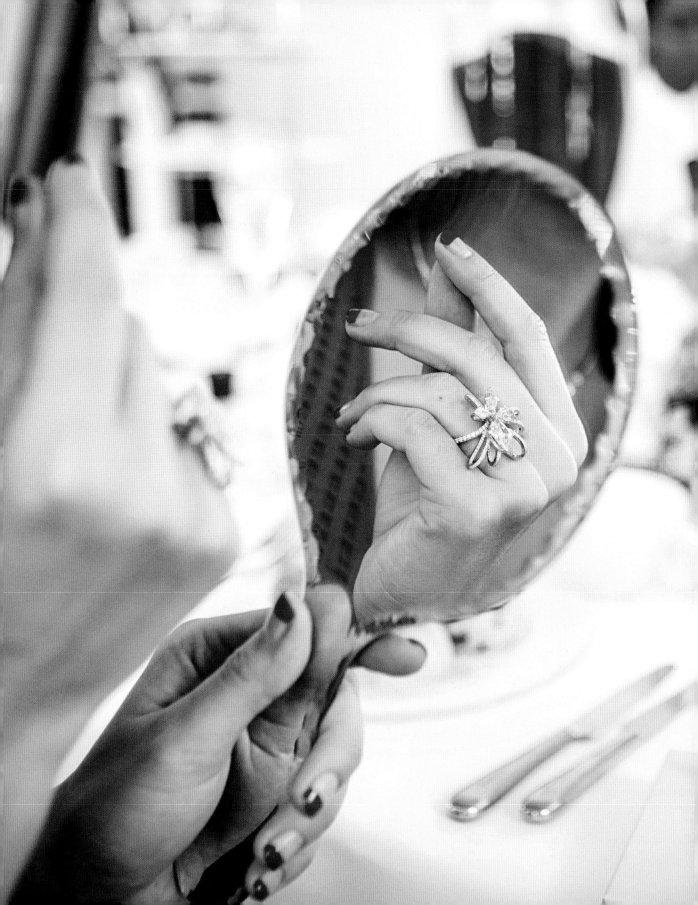

Draw inspiration from your mother's and grandmother's jewellery boxes and their old photographs. Their style is probably dissimilar to yours, but it can certainly give you fresh ideas on how to update your own jewellery box.

Most earrings are relatively small, but they will most likely be in the direct line of vision of anyone you talk to, so they should be carefully chosen. Consider what you want the earrings to do: complement your hair or your skin tone, or perhaps bring out your eye colour?

Even if you wear delicate and subtle jewellery on a daily basis, do give chunky jewellery a chance. Just one bigger piece can add a layer of playfulness to your jewellery style and make your presence more noticeable.

Coco Chanel wore a pair of matching Verdura Maltese cross cuffs almost on a daily basis, so why not find your own pair of signature cuffs? They could play the role of your personal armour and give you a feeling of great power.

You don't need a big diamond on your finger for your ring to be the talk of the party. Never underestimate the power of a striking cocktail ring, which is a great way to embellish an evening outfit. To keep the look elegant stick to a maximum of one ring on each hand. Make sure that your nails are well manicured, as a cocktail ring will be drawing attention to your hands.

Inspired by traditional Indian bridal jewellery, hand chains merge bracelets with rings, resulting in an enthralling hand adornment. A diamond-encrusted hand chain is one of the most luxurious pieces you could own, and its sparkle will surely captivate others as you move your hands. Alternatively, you could opt for a simple delicate gold hand chain to add a subtle glimmer to your hand.

It used to be seen as a fashion faux pas to mix different colours of metal, but I have always wondered why. Don't be afraid to mix your golds: they complement each other better than you think. Experiment and find the blend of colours that best suits your skin tone and hair colour.

If you care about where your clothes come from, extend the same courtesy to your jewellery. Before investing in a jewel, learn about its provenance: how and where it was manufactured and where the materials come from.

Discard the notion that jewellery must be costly in order to look impressive. Beautiful pieces of jewellery don't need to break the bank – even cheap jewellery can look grand if chosen carefully. Don't shy away from mixing fine and costume jewellery, as it can create an unusual look.

The majority of us are guilty of wearing the same earrings day in and day out, without giving a second thought to all the other earrings in the jewellery box. Have a thorough look through your collection, and set yourself a challenge to change your earrings every other day to add more excitement to your everyday look.

Organise your jewellery. Invest in a quality jewellery box with lots of little open compartments, which will help you to organise jewellery in the most efficient way and facilitate your daily jewellery choices.

Don't be embarrassed to ask even the most rudimental questions about jewellery to acquire new knowledge about this exciting world. It is very useful to know your stones and metals, especially when it comes to investment pieces.

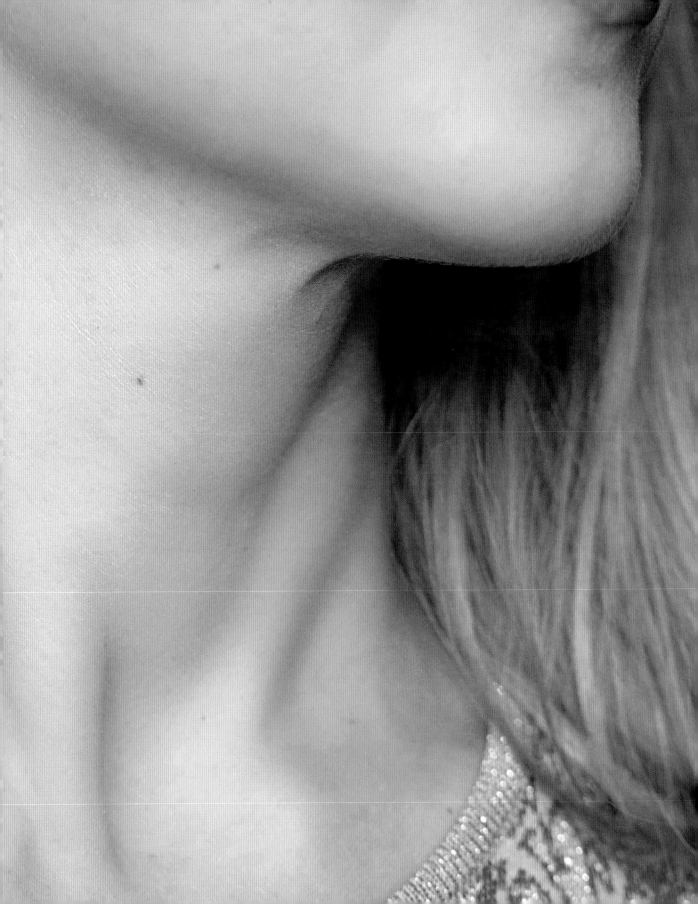

An engraving can add an intimate and meaningful touch to any piece of jewellery, be it an engagement ring or a simple locket necklace. Remember the cracker jack ring that Holly Golightly and her love interest had engraved at Tiffany's in *Breakfast at Tiffany's*?

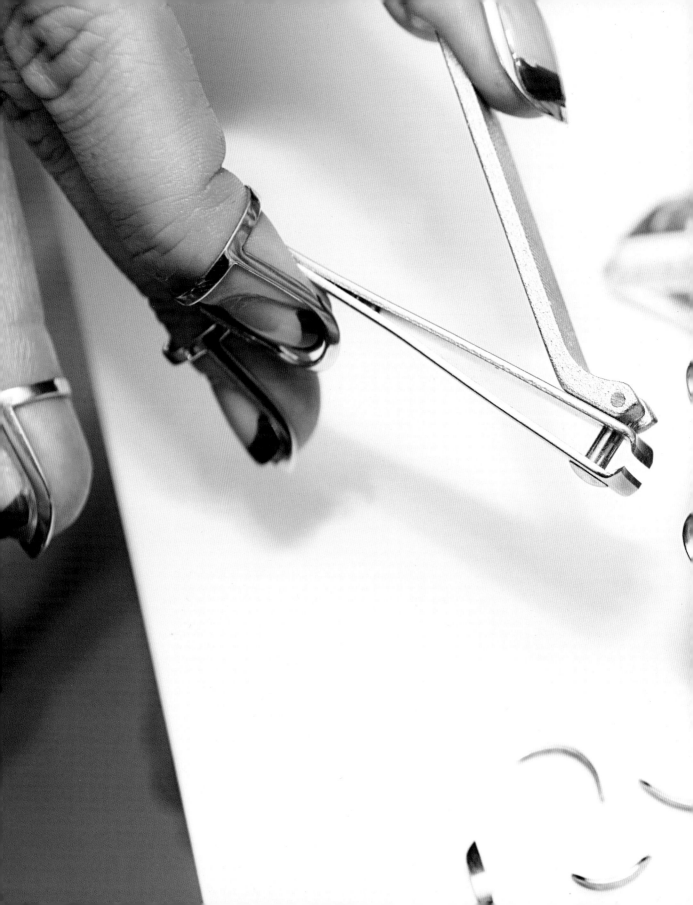

Chain, chain, chain! Go for a minimalist look by layering with a collection of simple but elegant chains – no pendants needed! These days, it's not unusual for jewellery designers to use standard chains instead of designing their own.

If it's not the right length, don't despair! Necklace extenders are wonderful things to keep in your jewellery box. Adding length to any necklace opens up a whole new level of layering and the compositions you can create.

Thank you James Smith, Julia Flit, Olga Nikolskaya, my fiancé Gustavo Medeiros and to all of my followers.
Thank you for your love, guidance and patience throughout.

British Library Cataloguing-in-Publication Data
A catalogue record for this book is available from the British Library.

The author and publisher gratefully acknowledge the permission granted to reproduce the copyright material in this book. Every effort has been made to trace copyright holders and to obtain their permission for the use of copyright material. The publisher apologises for any errors or omissions in the text and would be grateful if notified of any corrections that should be incorporated in future reprints or editions of this book.

Printed in China for ACC Art Books Ltd, Woodbridge, Suffolk, IP12 4SD, UK

www.accartbooks.com